You Can Do It Too!

APOSTLE CLARA GRIFFIN

The events in this book are portrayed to the best of Apostle Clara Griffin's memory. While all the stories in this book are true, some names and identifying details have been changed to protect the privacy of the people involved. The conversations in this book all come from the author's recollections, though they are not written to represent word-for- word transcripts, the essence of the dialogue is accurate. Writing In Faith aims to publish works of integrity and excellence, which is why this book has been offered to readers, however, the story, the experiences, and the words are the author's alone.

Scripture quotations are taken from the Holy Bible, King James Version

Published by: Writing In Faith
Baton Rouge, La.
www.writinginfaith.com
writinginfaith57@gmail.com

ISBN 978-0-9974047-7-7
0-9974047-7-9

Cover Design by: Aaron McBride ©2019
dbr.graphics

Editing by: Chermarlita M.
Lafayette
1love4holythree@gmail.com

Clara Griffin(text)
You Can Do It
Too!

Table Of Contents

Acknowledgements

I would like to take this opportunity; to express my gratitude. Several men, and women have been a great blessing to me. Therefore, I would like to honor them. Those individuals have been an inspiration to me in both my life, and ministry. The word teaches us to give honor; where honor is due. First, I thank God. He has entrusted me with his word. Secondly, "Disciples On Call Ministries" for their continual support, and prayers. My family, my three sons: Torrey, Kendall and Derrion Griffin. I love you, and I speak God's blessings over your lives. Apostle Larry Yarborough, Apostle Robert Cousin, Pastor Alverio Woodfork, and Evangelist Terry Williamson.

~Apostle Clara
Griffin~

Introduction

"You Can Do It Too" was birthed out of the trying of my faith, in a death to life situation. We as believers have been given power; to speak life into any dead situation. Christians should help other people of God, with their Christian journey. New believers should be properly taught concerning miracles, signs, and wonders. Miracles, signs, and wonders were not just for the generals of old, or the leaders of today. They were for every believer. My vision for this book was to enlighten everyone. The people of God can heal the sick; cleanse the lepers; and raise the dead. You are able to do all of these things. Jesus has given you the power, and authority to do so. Jesus says in John 14:12: *He that believeth on me, the works that I do shall he do also, and greater works than these he shall do, because I go to my Father.* In conclusion, we are able to operate in the same power as our Father did. We should see the manifestations from it; because, the Holy Spirit is working in us.

Preface

I would like to begin this book; by sharing part of my testimony with you. I believe it's important to know: what God can do in the life of a believer. *Then, they said to the Lord: "What shall we do; that we may work the works of God?" Jesus answered and said to them: "This is the work of God; that you believe in Him whom He sent* (John 6:28-29)."

I was born in Opelousas, LA. I accepted Christ at an early age. My church membership was with Ebenezer Baptist Church. I had sat under the leadership of Pastor Norlan Arvie. In 2007, I moved to Ruston, LA. There, I attended Miracle Temple Church of God in Christ, under the leadership of Superintendent Thomas Kennedy. While, I was there; I was taught more about the word of God. In 2009, I heard the voice of God speak to me. The Holy Spirit said: "ministry." Previously, I had a phone ministry; therefore, I thought that was my permanent ministerial calling. I did not realize: God was calling me into full- time ministry. Then, I moved back to Opelousas; where I attended The Truth Is Ministries. Shortly afterwards, I held my first conference. As a result, "Disciples On Call Ministries" was birthed out of that. I was ordained as a pastor, in June of 2014! Apostle Larry Yarbrough Sr. of Arkansas performed my ordination. In September of 2017, I was affirmed as an apostle by Apostle Larry Yarbrough!

Chapter 1

"The Beginning Of Ministry"

"You Can Do It Too" It is an eye catching title. As a result, it could incite you to think: What can I do? I want to take you on a spiritual journey into the word of God! We will learn: What we are able to do! If you want to experience more of God; you would want to continue reading. Nevertheless, if you have become comfortable where you are; stop reading, right here. Yes, I said it. Do not go any further; because, this will open your mind! You'll become susceptible to the unexpected, unbelievable, and unimaginable. If you are ready to go on this journey with me; let's go!

I was meditating one day. Suddenly, I heard in my spirit: " You Can Do It Too." Then, I thought: What can I do? I began to read the word of God. I was reminded that: I had used the same words; to minister to someone. I did not know: This was going to be a book! I have prayed for many people with various types of illnesses. Also, I have prayed for individuals, in other areas of their lives. However, God has never raised the dead through me. This was something I had read about, previously. Although, I never thought: I would be believing God to do it! You see a headache, backache, or finances were seemingly easy targets. I watched as God would do it; when, we came into agreement with the Word of God! Some were answered right away; albeit, with some of the prayers it was a process. There were times; when, it seemed like the prayers were unheard. Then, I would ask God: Why nothing happened with this one? What did we not do? Well, we soon realized that: we had received our answer. Sometimes, we may pray, and know what we are believing to happen. However, if it does not occur; we might begin to question our prayers. Although, it was answered; when, we first prayed. Nevertheless, it just wasn't the way; we expected. All things work together for the good of them that love God, and those who are the called according to his purpose. In other words, it will work out for our good. In order, for all of this to happen; our faith has to be increased by the power of God. Today, we can look at these; as we begin to understand we can do this too. We can be young, and tempted. Albeit, we can still live a life; pleasing to the Lord. To feel remorse for something means that: We did wrong, and we feel bad about it. Jesus was tempted of the devil for forty days! He was hungered, but he did not sin. Our Savior was offered the kingdom of Satan, and refused it as well. That lets us know temptations will come even in ministry, but we do not have to accept it. We may be offered a higher salary; to keep quiet about things going on with the leaders. We may be offered fame, and fortune. Nevertheless, we do not have to accept any of it. Jesus said he will make your name great, and he will supply all of our needs! Hence, we don't need to bow to Baal.

The sermon is to help us live out our God ordained lives. Our futures have already been planned for us by Christ. Jesus says we are blessed when we mourn, or remain humble. He is showing us his characteristics; these are some of the things he has already endured for us today. No matter who tells us of our mistakes, mess ups, or mishaps; we can do what Jesus did. There may be times; when we are badly treated, betrayed, or spat upon etcetera.

When that occurs; we need to forgive our trespassers. We must remain humble; because, Jesus will fight our battles for us. Persecution will come to every believer; because, we are threats to Satan, and his kingdom. Nevertheless, be steadfast and unmovable. We should always abound in the works of the Lord. Sometimes, it can be the hardest thing for some of us to do; because, we are trying to figure out things. We might ask ourselves: Why did this happen to me? Forgiving someone who has wronged us; can be hard for us. I have come to realize that the reason it's so hard is; because, we are operating in our flesh. Scripture says deny yourself take up your cross, and follow me. Well, to deny yourself means it's not about you anymore; you have taken up your cross for Christ's sake. Therefore, it's not about you anymore.

There are three things we will look at now: Suffering, sacrificing, and serving. We will suffer on this journey with the Lord, but it doesn't compare to the present glory. To suffer for Him would be; to reign with Him. Suffering sometimes will come in the form of people lying on us; talking about us; deceiving us; and trying to discredit us. However, God still says pray for our enemies, and love them. You might say: How am I supposed; to do this? They are trying to destroy me. Leaders might try to come against you, and talk about you to other leaders. As a result, you might feel betrayed. Beloved, if you are not operating in the flesh; your oppressors will not be able to move you. You might sacrifice spending time with your family, or friends. Sometimes, you might sacrifice buying yourself something; to help someone less fortunate. There are numerous homeless and hungry individuals. Putting clothes on someone else's back would be honorable.

Unfortunately, we occasionally find out some people really were not needy, at all. Therefore, they used you. What spirit were you operating in; when, you helped the individual? Serving the people of the community, family, and friends could be rewarding. Oftentimes, we do all; we can to meet their needs. It would be a slap in your face; to find out they only used you. The individuals might even talk about you to everyone. Now, you are angry. When you accept Christ as your personal savior; you have decided to take up your cross. Therefore, deny yourself and follow Christ!

When it becomes too much for you; you might be ready to quit. Jesus was not a quitter. We may never experience what Christ did, but we can operate like him! It's time to realize: What you have said yes to, by following Christ. Jesus says in (Mark 11:25-26 Amp): Whenever you stand praying, if you have anything against anyone forgive him, drop the issue, let it go so that your Father who is in heaven will also forgive you your transgressions, and wrongdoing against him and others, but if you don't forgive, neither will your Father in heaven forgive your transgressions. Drop the issue; let it go. Simply don't bother with it again; forget it even happened. No matter what they have done; let it go. Therefore, your sins may be forgiven. Unforgiveness can cause harm to your body. It can cause a plethora of health problems. Some individuals might have family problems. Others might even experience death. It is a silent killer to some. Bitterness, and resentment are two major blockers of blessings. God can not move in the midst of bitterness, and resentment. Unforgiveness keeps the fruit of the spirit; from operating in your life. It is contrary to faith working in your life as a believer.

Be free today knowing: You can do it too! John 14:12 says: *if we believe on Him; greater works we shall do* (paraphrase). All we have to do is believe on: What He has already done! The works are done by faith with the Holy Spirit working in us. How do I believe? Hebrews 11:1 says: *Now faith is the substance of things hoped for, and the evidence of things not seen.* Let's focus on Now faith is: It will work for us; as soon as, we begin to confess what has already been done. We don't have to wait for anything. All we have to do is believe: Now! It was already finished on the cross. The cross represents the workings of our Lord, and Savior. It exemplifies; what was done for us. The death, burial, and resurrection is what Jesus did for the believers.

I was a member of a ministry for 20 years. I watched my leader preach, teach, and live the word of God in his life. I took notes on his teachings. After church, I would go home, and study. Then, I would return for the next service. I did not realize; what was being taught. Albeit, the teachings resonated I could do it too! Previously, I thought only the pastor could make a difference. Albeit, he was supposed; to tell us about what he was able to do. "Greater works than these; he shall do." I can do greater works how is that? Jesus goes to the Father, on your behalf. Let me explain: When Jesus was with the disciples he was in the flesh. John 14:16 says: a*nd I will pray to the Father, and He shall give you another Comforter that he may abide with you forever.* The Comforter is the Holy Spirit; which resides with us always. When the Holy Spirit is working in us; He will lead, and guide us into all truth. The Holy Spirit will speak to us. God's spirit can show us things; we might not see with the naked eye. Jesus ended his teaching by saying: The people were astonished at His doctrine. Jesus taught them as one having authority, and not as a scribe.

It amazed people; to see that the law was no longer being taught. They were no longer under the curse. The people of God were freed! We can do the same with the authority, and power God has given us. Jesus taught sound doctrine. We must employ the Holy Spirit. We have not been called; to be recognized for popularity's sake. We are called, and chosen to represent Christ. We must teach; what He has taught. We are supposed; to say only what the Father says.

Nothing else should be added or subtracted. Let's stand, and take authority over the enemy. Let us fight back with the Word of God, and power.

Chapter 2

"Walking In Your God Given Authority"

Let's look at what Genesis 1:1 and 1:26-28 is saying: *In the beginning, God created the heavens and the earth.* Therefore, we know: We were integral components of God's plan. He then said: *"Let us make man in our image*; whose image reflects The Father, Son, and Holy Spirit." We are made in God's image, after His likeness. Therefore, we should look like God. Also, we should operate as the Lord does. We were created; to operate as Jesus does with the same power. Christians should exercise the same authority Christ did. He has given us the authority; to replenish, subdue, and have dominion. We have been called; to restore things back to its natural use.

God's Word gives us authority. You may say: This isn't for me. It was for the disciples. Some might say: This is my pastor's responsibility. It's surely not mine! We were given dominion! Our authority helps us; to replenish, and subdue. It was for all of mankind. All believers can conquer all evil, sickness, and attacks.Blood bought believers can have authority even over death! We are God's children; therefore, our authority over the earth is powerful! We can speak things into existence. Jesus needs a body to operate in; hence, we should receive The Holy Spirit. Once, we receive God's spirit; he can operate in and through us. We can now heal the sick; cleanse the lepers; and raise the dead. We can perform these acts by the empowerment of the Holy Spirit. All God said in Mark 11:23 was: *you speak to the mountain, and it shall move.* Wait, all I have to do is speak? The answer is yes! There is power in your mouth! However, you must be willing; to believe what you say.

I can remember; when, my mom expired in front of my family, and me. After, having tried CPR to no avail; we accepted she was gone. There was nothing; we could do. My family, and I did not recognize our holy power. We had a legal right; to rebuke death! We had a majestic ability; to speak life back into our mother. We did not activate our gifts! Years later, I learned of the power, and authority Jesus had given us. I was told about Adam and Eve. Therefore, I knew that: I could do it too! Unfortunately, I didn't understand, at that time. We can heal all manners of sickness, and disease. We have authority over unclean spirits, and we are able to cast them back to Hell. What an eye opener! We don't have to wait on the pastor, or accept the results of a bad diagnosis. Jesus has given us the same power; He has. Thank you, Jesus! I can do it too, according to the Word of God!

Having that attitude will change situations. Jesus did in Matt 8:5-9 to the Centurion. One word can change someone's life; a death sentence; or a diagnosis. All we have to do is speak it, and believe. The Centurion was a man of authority, and many answered to him. However, he didn't know of the power, so he went to Jesus for help. The

Centurion had faith in the work, and the Word. He had his trust in the right place, and his hope was in Jesus. Jesus told John's disciples to go, and tell John what they had seen, and heard. He was sending them to tell John faith was at work: The lame began; to walk. The blind embraced sight. Deaf ears were opened. Even the dead were raised!

Would that be possible; for us to do? By faith through the Holy Spirit, these are the miracles we can now do. Miracles, signs, and wonders shall follow them that believe. If you are a believer; you can operate in the same manner as Jesus did. We need faith to receive the Holy Spirit; to do what he did. We must realize only faith can speak to nothing, and make it something. It should excite us to begin to speak healing, deliverance, etc into existence, now. Ezekiel was told to speak to the dry bones. The bones had no skin, and they were not together. Nevertheless, Ezekiel obeyed God, and spoke to them! Scripture says: The skin appeared on the bones, and strength developed. Then, the bones began to come together. The bones became strong, and flesh developed on them. We can speak to any dead situation in our lives, and life will enter into it. Elijah caused it not to rain! He did, so by commanding the heavens to shut up, and be still! As a result, rain did not come. We say that the Lord is doing his work; when, the weather is bad. Albeit, we see we have power over the weather. We have power to change the report of bad weather, as well.

When Jesus was sleeping on the boat with his disciples; the wind became strong. The disciples became afraid. They awakened Jesus. He arose and rebuked the wind. Jesus said unto the sea: "Peace be still." As a result, the wind ceased. Then, he questioned the disciples about their cowardly behavior. Jesus said: "Don't you have any faith?" What Jesus was saying to them was: He had already taught them; what they were able to do! He had equipped the disciples. Nevertheless, they were still afraid to do it. Jesus had walked with the disciples for a long time. However, they were still dependent on him; to do the work. Jesus' works were demonstrated; before, them. Therefore, as long as he was with them; they had a hard time doing the work.

Now, you must do this in faith without doubting, or being moved by what you see. Believing, and trusting in the word of God is: All he wants us to do! Jesus said: *When you pray believe; you have received. But without faith it is impossible to please God* (Hebrews 11:6). *For he that cometh to God must believe that he is, and a rewarder of them that diligently seek him.*

God will reward you for believing in him, and being consistent. Jesus asked a question: Before, my return will you find faith on the earth? He was not looking at how good we sound, or how we dress. Jesus was not concerned about: How many people were there! He wanted; to see faith at work. Some miracles took a long time; to manifest. Others seemed like they would never take place. Nevertheless, we believed. When you plant a seed in the ground; you don't know what's going to happen. All you are doing is expecting; to see the plant sprout up from the substance that was planted, right? Well, that's the same way faith works. You don't know the outcome, and all you physically see is what is, before you. Albeit, you are continually believing for a favorable harvest!

Let's look at the beginning, and how the authority was given: First, God said let us make man in our image. In whose image was man created? We were created; to reflect attributes of the Father, Son, and Holy Spirit. Then, the Lord said: "Let them have dominion over." Then he told them to be fruitful, and multiply. Man was instructed; to replenish the earth, and subdue. Hence, we are made in God's image.

Albeit, we have been given authority; to subdue the earth. It was already predestined for us. When Adam disobeyed God; it was stripped from him. Now, the second Adam (Jesus) came, and bridged the gap for us. Where the law once was effective; we are no longer, under the law. We are saved by grace. We were thought of; before, we were formed in the wombs of our mothers. No longer, do we have to wait on anything. We can do the same things Jesus did on earth.

Now, we can do what: Jesus taught his disciples to do. We can! In John 5:19, Jesus said: *Verily, Verily I say unto you; the Son can do nothing of himself, but what he seeth the Father do; for whatever He doeth, these also doeth the Son.* We should only be doing; what the Father has done. To expect the supernatural, miraculous, signs, and wonders; is not out of the ordinary. That was the ministry of Jesus. Let's not get so relaxed people of God! We should not just sit around, and accept what the enemy throws at us. Although, nobody might be saying anything about it, or teaching on it. Let's begin to believe, and expect. The Holy Spirit is our helper, teacher, and guide.

Therefore, we are not alone. Once, we are saved, and filled, we receive help. As a result, we can operate as Jesus did! Poverty, death, and sickness have no power. In the Name of Jesus, demons tremble! The power is in his name; all we have to do is use it. When, we do it the Bible's way; we will always get good results!

Chapter 3

"The Journey Begins"

In this chapter, I want to talk more about faith at work; your will; and you can do it too. In life, we are faced with many challenges. There are times; we want to give up, and shut the door on God. I want to restore your desire; your trust; and your faith. I want to bring you back to the place; where you once were. For those who do not know how to believe; I want to open your heart, and minds. The supernatural world is real. I want to share a personal story with you about the death, and life of a believer. How often do believers come together in faith; to believe God for the impossible?

I had met a lady; who was very ill. She came to visit the ministry with expectations. The woman believed: The Lord was going to do something for her. She was determined; not to leave without an encounter with the Lord. As we began to worship; the Lord showed me her body lying in a casket. Then, I went over to her, and laid hands on her. I cancelled the spirit of death off of her. After the service, we had conversed. She said: she would be back. Well, she did come back for Bible Study. I was teaching on unforgiveness that night. After the service, she had asked me questions about the teaching. I told her the damages; it could cause to us. There are times; when, people might hurt us. Sometimes, we go through abuse in our lives. As a result, we can begin to form resentment, and bitterness in our heart towards our oppressors. If we do not get delivered; it can cause so much damage to us. We must be careful. We may hold the unforgiveness in our hearts, but it damages us more. Most of our trespassers have forgotten our mere existences. Cancer, high blood pressure, depression, or death could develop from bitterness, and resentment. This spirit is determined to take you down.

Once, we forgive our enemies; we can

embrace deliverance. Once, we become delivered from it all; we will feel so much better. Then, we can move forward in our lives. The lady who had visited my church began to tell me; she was dealing with the spirits of bitterness and unforgiveness. She wanted to be delivered from those strongholds. Then, I began to minister to her one on one. God delivered her, and she was able to forgive her oppressors. This lady was also diagnosed with cancer, and was taking medicine for it. After, her deliverance she began to feel so much better! Her healing took place; as a result, she became cancer free. She testified that the doctor told her she did not need her medication on a constant basis anymore. As she continued to visit; she became a member of the ministry. Her faith began to grow in God, even more. As time progressed; she began to have stomach pain. We prayed about it to no avail. She did not get relief from it. She went back to the doctor. After several treatments, she was diagnosed with cancer, once more. Only this time, her faith was increased; to believe for her healing.

She believed that: She could do it too! We began to believe God for her healing. We stayed focused on the word of God, through it all. My member's strength began to return. Therefore, my member was able to testify of God's goodness. The Lord had kept her through so much. Also, he brought her out of her hardships. She continued to confess the word of God, over her life. She shared personal stories of the things; she had endured on her journey. I had asked the question: If death would meet us here; where would we be? She pondered; then, met me in the office. Enthusiastically, she answered me. Frequently, we talked and prayed together. I watched this flower beautifully bloom. This lady knew God for herself. Nevertheless, she had no idea of what; we had power to do in Christ.

As we journey on with the Lord; our faith should be increased! We should be excited about the outcome of what faith brings. Now faith is the substance of things we hope for, and the evidence of things not seen. We don't have to see it. Jesus says: Unless, you see a sign you won't believe, and that's not faith. Jesus wants us to trust him; even when, we can't trace him. He wants us to believe him, for what seems impossible. God's word says all things are possible; to those who believe. All we have to do is believe; what his word says. Faith is the key; to all that we need from the Lord. All we have to do is see it in the Spirit. You may have the skills, and the money. However, faith, and favor will open the door for you. Faith becomes the substance, of what you don't see. You might have received a bad report, and you are experiencing the symptoms from it. However, by faith, you begin to speak the word over it. Continue to walk it out, no matter what. See faith does not lose; no matter what the situation looks like. God sees your faith even, until the end. Sickness cannot override the contents of the Bible; unless, you give Satan permission. Do not allow doubt, fear, or worry entry into your life! Faith becomes what you do not see, but what you are expecting. The expectation of what we do not see is: What keeps us excited, and helps us to keep going. You may not see yourself healed, delivered, or blessed, etc. Albeit, with faith, and expectation it's already done; because, you have spoken it. You are not entitled to it; unless, you see it. I can have it;

before, I actually have it in my possession. I can possess it, by faith! Now, we are on a journey of doing it too....

Chapter 4

"The Process OF Faith"

Now, faith is the substance (evidence, assurance) of things hoped for, and the evidence of things not seen. We are simply saying: We believe what we do not see! As we walked this process out; we were believing God for healing. It didn't matter what the doctors were saying, or what we were seeing with her. We continued to believe that: God was going to answer us. She began to speak words of life over herself. When we are walking in faith; we must be careful of the words we speak. We can't say we are healed, and continue to say we are sick. We can not welcome pain, or embrace not feeling well. All we would be doing is nullifying God's word. Our words must be in line with the Lord's. God says it's impossible; to please him without faith. We understand the world was formed, and framed, by the word of God. Likewise, things which are seen; were not made of things which do appear. By faith Enoch was translated; that he may not see death. A spoken word was in existence here, and it manifested. We need faith to please God; there is no other way. The trying of your faith worketh patience! Hence, it may not happen; when, you expect it to manifest.

Prayerfully, if you hold on; you will see the manifestations take place in the situation. Our minds have to be transformed; in order, to understand faith. It is not something for you to believe only; because, someone said it! No, that is not the case! It is changing; the way you think. Our minds must continually be renewed. Be not conformed to this world, but be transformed by the renewing of your mind. The world's way is what we were taught, and we have adapted to that mindset. Once, we are saved; we should begin to read the word of God. It would change our way of thinking, and doing things. We were formed in the image of Christ, after his likeness. We were formed, before the fall of man. Once, the fall of man (sin) entered into the world; man's mind became contaminated. Jesus came, and bridged the gap for us. He became a ransom for us on the cross. We are no longer under the law (curse); we are under grace. We have a way out of sin by accepting Jesus Christ, as our Savior. Jesus began to teach, and demonstrate how things were supposed to be. Then, he sent The Holy Spirit to aid us.

When God created Adam; he breathed into his nostrils the breath of life and man became a living being (Gen2:7). The breath of God is the Holy Ghost. Job said: "The Spirit of God has made me, and the breath of the Almighty gives me life." The moment God breathed breath into Adam; he came alive. When Adam opened his eyes; the first contact he had was with the Holy Spirit. He was the breath; that flowed through Adam's body. He remained hovering over him. Adam stood up completely; filled with the presence of God. The scripture says that God, The Holy Spirit was the power of creation. The Holy Spirit adorned the heavens (Job 26:13). God wants to pour his spirit on you. He wants to breathe his spirit into you. He wants you, to be like Adam; to come alive!

The Holy Spirit is our teacher, helper and guide. How does the Holy Spirit speak? He witnesses to your very conscience. Paul said to the church at Rome: "I tell you the truth in Christ. I am not lying; my conscience also, bears witness with me in the Holy Spirit." You should never doubt the leading of the Holy Spirit. At a time, when your inner man is troubled; don't move. If you attempt to be your own guide; you will literally collapse. Listen to God's voice; as it speaks to your very soul. When, I heard the words: "You Can Do It Too;" I knew it was the Holy Spirit speaking. He spoke clearly. I just did not know; it was for a book. I continued to pray, and ask what was the purpose of the sentence. As a result, I heard a book. Well, here it is! Would you truly; like to discern The Holy Spirit's voice? Okay, read these profound words: The Spirit Himself bears witness with our spirits; that we are children of God. How do you know; it's true? His Spirit bears witness with our spirit. The Holy Spirit is God, the witness. Peter said: we are witnesses to these things.

Also, The Holy Spirit is given to those; who are obedient (Acts 5:23). We must repent (turn away) from the old man, or the old way of doing things. We should put on the new man. In order for, that to happen; we must accept Christ. We must begin to walk out; what he has set before us. Scripture says: *Be not conformed to this world, but be transformed by the renewing of your mind, so you may prove what is that good, acceptable, and perfect will of God.* Your mind has to be changed from your old way of thinking. Walking in faith is like walking with a blindfold on; we can't see it . However, we know it's there, so we do all we can to get to it. Our faith will be tried in the fire, whether it be in family, marriage, health, etc. We must continue to profess the word of God over it, and confess it out of our mouths. We must believe that it will change; in spite of, what it looks like.

This lady believed; in spite of, what she was going through in life. She didn't allow it; to shake her faith. There were many that questioned our faith; because, of what they were seeing in her. Nevertheless, that didn't stop us. The Bible says faith without works is dead; well, that meant we had to do something. We refused to sit around, and accept a diagnosis without even trying to stand on the Word. See when you have the word on the inside of you; you should begin to confess it over the situation. The enemy will fight you on every hand; you must continue to do what Jesus did. Speak the word, and he will flee. Elijah did not listen to the woman; who said she only had enough for her, and her son to eat. If Elijah would have listened; the woman, and her son would have died. That's exactly; what would have happened. Instead, Elijah gave the woman instructions. The woman obeyed, so she was able to see the manifestation of the spoken word. Elijah spoke a word, and believed that it would come to pass. The woman received the word, and they watched it manifest. Now, one spoke and they both believed, God gave the increase to it.

When we speak a word in faith; we cannot turn back from our confession. We can not discount our confessions; because, of what it looks like. Also, we see we must continue to believe; what we confessed would take place. This woman only saw; what was in her hand.

Elijah saw what was in the hand of God, and that's what made the difference. The power that we have been given; is the same power Jesus had. Jesus had that power; when, he spoke to the devil. Jesus healed blinded eyes; he caused the lame to walk; the deaf to hear; and the dead were raised. That same power occurred; when, Jesus hung on the cross. He bled, died, and was resurrected from the dead. Yes, that same power lies within us; today, we just have to operate in it by faith. We have been given power; to heal the sick. We can give sight to the blind, and can heal all manners of sickness and disease. Believers can even raise the dead! Yes, God has given us that kind of powcr! So you see; sometimes, things look a certain way. As a result, we may think things won't change. Just speak to it, and watch what may happen. If you are wondering: You can do it, too! Yes, you have the son of God. You are a born again believer. You can do it, too: Jesus said to them; who believe. All you have to do is believe in the Lord, and what he has said. You can operate just like Jesus did.

Jesus sent word to Hezekiah; to tell him to get his house in order. Hezekiah turned his face to the wall, and began to speak the Word to: the Word! It had an effective turnaround. See when the Word heard the Word; it responded. John 1:1 says: *In the beginning was the Word, and the Word was with God, and the Word was God.* See the Word spoke, and the response was with the Word. The woman with the issue of blood for 12 years came into contact with the Word, and it stopped immediately. When the Word shows up; things must change: Sickness can't stay. Poverty can't stay, wickedness can't stay, no it must change. Whatever mountain is in your way all you have to do is speak to it and it will move. See how awesome this is! You have power; to speak to a mountain! Mountains come in various forms: lack, depression, fear, debt, or even death. Speak to it; what Jesus said! It will move. As believers, we have access to whatever; Jesus had access to, also! He did not leave us alone; he left us the Comforter (Holy Spirit). The Holy Spirit lives on the inside of believers, and will lead and guide us. Also, He will teach us, and help us. Whatever we need the Holy Spirit is our help. Therefore, there is no need to fear anything on this journey. We have love, power, and a sound mind; that has been given to us. Now, it's time to use the power, and authority that has been given to us! Come on, you can do It too!

Chapter 5

"The Outcome Of Faith"

For I am not ashamed of the Gospel of Jesus Christ, for it is the power of God unto salvation to everyone that believes, to the Jew first, and also to the Greek. For therein is the righteousness of God revealed from Faith to Faith: as it is written, the just shall live by Faith. (Romans 1:16-17).

When, we began this journey with the lady; we didn't look at how long it would take. We did not know; if God was going to answer us. We did not know; what people would say. We began with the expectation; that God would grant us our request. His righteousness will be revealed; when, we begin to see it! We must see it; before, we receive it! Someone once said you can't have it; unless, you see it. You must see it in the spirit first by Faith. When we were believing God to heal this lady; she continued to decline instead of getting better. What encouraged us; to keep going was her faith. We visited and prayed with her. As we spoke; I asked her if she was ready to go, and be with the Lord. Then, I had asked her; if she wanted to live. She continued to say: " I want to live." She continued to believe God; to heal her.

In spite of, all that she was dealing with; the Lord was helping her! In the months ahead, she began to decline even more. However, faith kept us going. She began to confess: She was healed by faith, and she would live. We began to hold miracle, and healing services. During that time, we were expecting God to move, and in many ways he did for many people. Her condition worsened, and she was taken to the hospital. After examining her, the family was called in for a meeting. The family made the final decision on her. Later that day, she went to be with the Lord. All seemed lost, and God had not answered us. She was gone, now what? Later that night, I had asked the Lord: What happened? I heard God say: Jesus died in 3 days.

Also, he resurrected. Well, what was the Lord saying to me? I had called a few people, and told them what I had heard. I told them that: Jesus had raised the dead. Therefore, we can to! They said: they were in agreement with me. They were willing; to support whatever, I had wanted to do! I began to pray, and read the word of God. When, I read that Jesus had already raised the dead; I decided that we would try it, too! As a result, I spoke with everyone. We began to pray the word of God, and expected him to do it. Now, we knew that we would be criticized, or talked about by others. However, not from leaders or their children. One could only assume that they would know; if they were preaching, and teaching the word. Now, we realize that is not always the case. Just because you have read something has happened; doesn't mean you believe it could happen for you. As a result, we began to pray in agreement.

The week rapidly progressed. It seemed like nothing was happening; oh, but the joy of faith. During the process of prayer, we continued to believe God with expectation. We went to the mortuary, and repeatedly prayed for a

43

miraculous resuscitation. Finally, the day of the funeral materialized. We prepared for the raising of the dead on that day, with expectation. Nevertheless, we did not see any results. We showed up early at the church. We fervently prayed, once more. Our prayers were prayed with expectation, for our demised sister to be raised. Well, the service started, and God's word was preached. Then, the morticians went on; to bury the demise. No, the dead was not resurrected. However, the faith of the people was definitely revitalized. We watched as the people left with, so much expectation! They were overflowing with joy! They had found out; what they could do.

In the beginning, it sounded like we had lost our minds! We stayed positive all the way through the funeral. After the preaching, the people had a reason; to believe for more. I can remember having heard people say: "They are crazy! What do they mean? Are they expecting her to arise?" Yes, we were expecting a miracle! The attendees had no idea that it was possible; because, they had never heard of it. Now, they were hearing something for the first time, and the excitement of it all pushed us even the more. Even though, the burial had taken place; I still sought answers. I still had these thoughts: "What happened here? Why wasn't she raised? Why weren't we heard?" Well, a few weeks later, my questions were answered. I was conversing with one of the believers. She had mentioned to me; what the Lord had revealed to her about our beloved departed sister in Christ. She said to me that the Lord had allowed her; to hear a conversation between him, and our demised friend. The Lord allowed her to see our deceased sister, as well. She said she heard the Lord ask our departed sister; if she wanted to come back to Earth. Before, our deceased sister in Christ answered; God showed her something. Then, she said no.

Well, there was my answer; she had a choice. She said: no. God could not go against her will. The peace I was left with was indescribable. You may say: "Why wasn't she healed?" Our sister had a choice. Therefore, God could not override it. We are waiting on God to do some things in our lives. Some people are waiting for God; to come, and change the world.

Some are waiting for God; to stop all the violence. Well, God has given you the authority to do that! He will only be coming back for his bride (church). God has given you, and I the authority. It is time; we began to use it. People may say all kinds of things; when, you are believing for something to happen in faith. Nevertheless, you must remember: You got saved in faith, and you received the Holy Spirit in faith! Am I correct? Okay, I had thought so! Therefore, we must do it all in faith! We must walk by faith, and not by sight. Only Faith can speak to nothing, and make it something. It might seem like all hope is gone, and there is nothing that can be done. However, if you begin to speak to it; you will began to see change. Albeit, if you just sit around looking at it; it will not change. The words you speak will bring life; to what was dead. God told Ezekiel to prophesy to the dry bones, and as Ezekiel obeyed, the bones came together. Speak to the dry places in your life. All you have to do is speak the word, and it will produce what you speak. People of God, it is time to begin to walk out; on what has already been placed on the inside of you. Allow

Faith to push you to a place; you have never been.

Chapter 6

"Going With God"

Verily, verily I say unto you, Except a corn of wheat fall into the ground and die, it abide alone, but if it die, it bringeth forth much fruit (John 12:24).

There are some things in our lives; that must die. Then, we could truly live, and continue to grow. Unfortunately, our sister in Christ died. Although, having watched faith literally grow in the people; after the fact, was the real blessing. The people were taken to a place; they had never been! In fact, they did not know the place even existed. Going to church, or reading the Bible isn't enough for some people. They began to look for demonstrations, and wanted to know that it happened to someone. We must begin; to walk out God's word by faith! As believers, we should begin to do; what we have been given the authority to do. As a result, people would begin to believe, and not just agree. We must not just be hearers of the Word of God; we must be doers of the Word, also. We must begin to walk out in God's Word in faith; if we are to follow Jesus. The seeds in our lives must die, so we may live. Seeds of abandonment, rejection, pain, hurt, lack, and depression must flee! Then, healing, and restoration can take place. We must first allow those negative things to die; then, we will see healing, and deliverance take place in our lives.

There are some situations; that we want to just forget about, or not discuss. Ironically, those are the important things. We should talk about those things. Then, we can forgive, repent and turn from those bad seeds. Positive seeds will manifest, as a result. Unforgiveness, as I stated earlier, is something that would impede our growth in God. We might be choosing to hold on to a bad relationship, or marriage. First of all the relationship, or marriage was probably not ordained by God. However, we embarked upon those situations; because, we did not want to be alone. Therefore, we chose to settle. Let it die, so the new growth can begin to flourish. Stop holding on to dead weight in your life, or ministry. If individuals want to leave; let them go! Just keep them in prayer, but keep moving forward. Jesus didn't stop loving us in our messes, but he didn't allow us to stop him from his assignment. Once it is dead; then, you will see the blessing in it. Scripture says much fruit. The weak flesh demised. Nevertheless, when we came together in prayer; the fruit was produced. Although, our sister in Christ is not physically here; the fruit is still producing daily.

The people had read about what Jesus had done, but didn't know it was for them to do as well. Their faith has grown, and now they know they can believe God for the impossible. The corrupted seeds had to die. Seeds of: unbelief, doubt, and fear all had to die. As a result, faith can go to work. The faith of the people has grown through all of this. Now, they can go on believing for more. Jesus showed up, and called Lazarus forth with authority. The power of the anointing destroyed the yoke of death. It had to release Lazarus. How did it happen? The word that was spoken; freed

Lazarus from the jaws of death. Scripture says the power of life, and death are in the tongue. Nevertheless, it won't work; if you don't say anything.

The Centurion man went to Jesus, for him to heal his servant. He knew Jesus' mere spoken words; would heal his servant. How powerful are our words; when, we speak with assurance! Praise God! It's not the confidence we have in ourselves; it's the confidence we have in Jesus! He will back it up; when, we speak! The word clearly states greater works than these; you shall do. We are able to do greater; when, the Holy Spirit is working in us. God watches over his word. He does not tend to tears, complaints, worry or fear. His words can not perform ill results. The Word is manifested; when, we speak in faith. Jesus wants us; to believe in him! We must speak in faith! Wavering doubtful words must cease. Stand on what you believe! The Bible is your platform! The scripture says miracles, signs, and wonders shall follow them that believe. You will begin to see miracles take place; as you continue to believe.

I can remember being approached by a demon spirit. The spirit spoke to me, and tried to put fear in me. The demon told me: "You had better not go to sleep." Well, I told that spirit: "If you come near this door; the Holy Ghost will meet you there!" Guess what? That spirit came under subjection; because, I showed no fear. I had spoken with authority. We don't have to fight, or fuss. All we have to do is: speak with authority. I believed what I spoke would take place, and it did! We should be the same way; when, we are believing God to validate us! I was asked; to pray for this woman about demons attacking her daughter. I invited her to the church. I had called in a few other people; to assist me. We prayed for about forty-five minutes, or an hour to no avail. The demons laughed at me, and began to talk to me, also. I did not show any fear. I commanded the demons to come out, and release its hold on the woman. The demons laughed even more. Nevertheless, we continued to pray, and called on the name Jesus. Eventually, the demons were casted out of the mother. See the demon was disguising itself in the daughter; where it was actually in the mother. Wow, that was deep! We stood in agreement; commanding with authority for the demon to relinquish its hold. The evil spirit complied. Had we given up; fear would have cancelled our victory. When you are faced with situations don't fear. Jesus did it; you can do it too. Jesus casted out many demons, and he also taught his disciples to do the same. It is also for us, today. It's time for us to walk in the authority; that has been given to us.

Once, you see that it works; you can do it, also! You will be ready; to deal with whatever comes your way! Why? The answer is: You will know God will back you up; when, you operate by faith. Faith opens doors that have been closed; faith will move mountains out of your way. All you have to do is believe. When our demised friend was buried; we did not forget about her. What we had experienced helped us; to prepare to continue to expect a miracle. It would have been easy for us to give up, and turn back on God. However, we could not, so much had taken place. The fruit of what we had done was visual. Whenever, something happens now; they are able to speak life into the situation.

I once read a story about an epidemic of a disease. The disease had infected 30 to 40 people. The doctors had no explanation for it. The man of God was a believer, and believed in healing. After, having read what Jesus had done; he believed he could do it too! He was called over to pray for the lady; whom was dying. The man of God had met the doctor there; who was pacing the floor. The doctor did not know; what else he could do. After all, 40 people had died from the disease, and now, another person was sick. The young believer walked up to the lady, and soon realized this was an attack of Satan. God had nothing to do with this. He then told the mother she will live, and the fever broke! Immediately, the young lady sat up, and ate. Her brother was also healed of that same plague. The believer prayed fearlessly for the 30-40 people that died. He could not understand why:They were not healed. Albeit, he did not stop believing; he continued to pray. As a result, God answered his prayer. Many were healed thereafter.

See we can't stop; because, we didn't get the results we were expecting. We must continue to believe God for a miracle. In that case, it was for a healing. Nevertheless, it may be for a breakthrough in finances. Another individual might be in prayer for a loved one; to be freed from jail. Someone else might need freedom from sickness. Don't you stop believing, and professing the Word of God! No matter how long it takes; it will work. We must continue to look to Jesus; whom is the author, and finisher of our faith. Jesus will see us through; he will watch over his word to perform it. He said he will never leave us, nor will he forsake us. The word of God is truth, and life. All we have to do is continue on our journey. Do not lose focus. Remain persistent, and you will get the results you are expecting.

Chapter 7

"From Death To Life"

Verily, verily I say unto you, He that heareth my word, and believeth on him that sent me, hath everlasting life, and shall not come into condemnation, but is passed from death to life (John 5:24).

We are faced with death daily. Not to mention, it is a tragedy; when, it occurs. Whether it's a sudden death, or a prolonged one still it hurts. There is still hope; when, we die in Christ. There are promises to us even in death. We will not be condemned; when, we hear and believe. Faith cometh by hearing, and hearing the word of God. Scripture says: we must hear and believe Jesus words. It's easy to see a situation, and believe it will not work. Nevertheless, we should apply the word, and begin to believe what it says.

We will get the results of what; we believed for, in prayer. We will have everlasting life that means: eternity with the Father. We will pass death; to receive life. To be absent from the body is to be present with the Lord. When we die as a believer in Christ; we will spend eternity with the Father. O death, where is thy sting. O grave, where is thy victory. The sting of death is sin, and the strength of sin is the law. Thanks, be to God; which gives us the victory through our Lord Jesus Christ. Death has no sting and the grave no victory. You are not dead; you are asleep in Christ.

As a believer, you have the victory. This is how much Jesus loves us. He will not allow death; to become our final outcome. When someone is deceased; we go and visit the gravesite. However, only a shell of the body is there. The dearly departed loved one is with the Lord as: He promised. We should rejoice; when, a believer goes to be with the Lord. We should find solace in knowing: They have kept the faith, and continued to believe. Faith at work in your life will produce patience. That means: we don't have to fear death. We should just expect to be with the Lord. During the process of death to life with our demised loved one; we continued to operate by faith. Even in death, we were able to rejoice; because, she was a believer. Therefore, she was going to have everlasting life. As a result, death had no sting, and the grave no victory. The shell (body) returned back to Earth. Albeit, her soul went to Heaven. Victory belongs to the believer in every area of our lives. Even though, our expired sister in Christ chose not to come back; we still got the victory. She is no longer sick, frail, or hurting. Our beloved sister is now healthy, whole, and full of life. Faith enabled us to come together, and believe for the impossible. We came together, and did what many didn't know was possible. In fact, most people did not know: It could be done. This is the faith that: Jesus is seeking.

We should have a faith that: will not give up or turn back to darkness. Our faith should indicate; if Jesus did it I can do it too. We can't say the word doesn't work, or Jesus doesn't answer prayers. We must try, and keep on trying. In walking with the Lord; he has given us a choice, and a will. We have a permissive will: Even if we know the Lord has said something; he will not force us to do it. He will leave that to us. Now, if we obey The Holy Spirit, we can expect good results. Unfortunately, if we are disobedient; we will get negative results. The blame would not be on God. He knows what's best for us; his plan has an expected favorable end. We have a favorable future; when, we are in God's perfect will. Life can throw us some blows, but all we have to do is hold fast to our faith.

Now, that we know we can do it too; we should be ignited to go deeper in the things of God. Jesus was accused of blasphemy; he was stoned; mocked and spat upon, etc. Nevertheless, he continued to trust in the Father that he would not be left alone. Jesus came to Earth on an assignment, and did not allow himself to be distracted by anything. He obeyed Father God's command, and he succeeded death. As a result, the victory became his. In spite of, not having enough; a bad diagnosis; being ridiculed; mocked; lied upon; or having been wrongly accused; keep the faith. Profess the Word of God, daily over the situation. Watch God move in your favor. Now, let's begin to walk by faith, and not by sight. Therefore, we may find favor from the Lord. Let's stop waiting on the Lord to come back; to heal; deliver, or bless us! Let's go out, and not let the workings of Jesus be in vain. "You Can Do It Too!"

In Conclusion

The lives of the people were changed forever. They embraced the fact that: they could make a difference in their own situations or in someone else's. They looked forward to doing even more. After, walking out the process of faith we can look back at the fruits; that were produced. There were some; who said their faith had never been so high! Now, they are expecting God to show up for them; when, they pray. They have had financial issues; sickness in their bodies; and problems on their jobs. Previously, they would complain, or settle for what was being done. Now, they have learned to apply the Word to the situation. It's time that: we stop telling people how big our problems are. We must begin to tell them how big our God is! The testimony of how God had healed tumors was phenomenal! Some individuals had gone to the doctor, and had negative reports. Some of those tests' results miraculously changed! When the people went back to the doctor; what had been seen was no longer there! They were excited about sharing their good news!

Once, we come into contact with the true and living God; we should begin to apply his word. Hence, we will always come out victorious. We no longer have to wish things were different, or wish we could change things. We can transform circumstances; all we have to do is speak the Word. God's Word in faith will turn a divided marriage into a marriage of unity. Lack can transform into prosperity. A terminal diagnosis that: resonates there is nothing we can do would change! God will say: "You will live and not die." Speaking the Word, and believing it will change it for you. You are already a winner! You are more than a conqueror! You're the head and not the tail! You are above only and not beneath! You are healed, delivered, and set free! You're no longer bound to the world's way of thinking, or doing. It's time that you begin to set your own atmosphere. Stop allowing the enemy to tell you what you can't do, or what you can't have. He can not determine; where you can not go! Your Heavenly Father has already predestined a life for you.

Jesus told Noah to build an ark. it was going to flood. The people thought Noah was crazy. Many did not believe; because, they saw no rain. Nevertheless, Noah continued to obey God. Another example would be; when, God told Mary she would have a son. She was instructed; to name him Jesus. Mary could not believe it was so; because, she had not been with a man. Joseph wanted to embarrass her, but the angel spoke to him concerning the matter. Then, Jesus said he must go away, but he would send The Comforter. They said: no However, he rebuked that, and kept the promise. I said that; because, Noah warned the people. God sends us warnings. Sometimes, we don't see it. We don't believe it; tragedy strikes. Then, we might begin; to question God. Unfortunately, it would be too late!

When Jesus came; he ripped the veil from top to bottom. We no longer have to go to the priest; to get our prayers through to God. We can go directly to The Father; when, we are in a relationship with him. The people are so quick to run to the pastor, or friends to get a prayer through for them. They do not know: they have the same access to Jesus. Mary's pregnancy was so uncommon to man, but not to God. If we were to hear of: the dead being raised; cancer healed without treatment, or someone getting released from a life sentence; we would say it's not true. Where is our faith? We say with our mouths that: we believe. However, when it's time; we look surprised. This is so; because, we really did not believe. We just said: what we heard others say. Church, it is time; to come out the box. What seems impossible to man; is possible with God. Man can not comprehend out of his natural mind, the things in the spirit. All things are possible to them; who believe. He said: All Things. Hence, it doesn't matter; how it looks. Also, it doesn't matter; how it sounds. It's possible. If Jesus said it; it is written. Therefore, you can do it. Walk out the promises; God has for you! No matter what it looks like; you can do it too!

Dedication

I have dedicated this book to three women of faith: These three ladies collectively acted; as a bridge that helped me to crossover from fear to faith. All three of these precious women battled the disease called cancer. However, they never lost their faith, love, or hope in God. They taught me to strongly stand in the midst of storms.

 My mom, Mrs. Flora Griffin was a very courageous woman; who never gave up, under no circumstances. My mother never stopped trusting God, no matter what! She faced many trials. Albeit, Flora Griffin continued; to keep the faith.

My friend, Johnny Ruth was a woman of faith, wisdom, and courage. When, I began my journey with the Lord; she would sit me down, and tell me about her faith in God. Johnny shared with me the trials; she faced in her life. Even when things were seemingly hopeless; Johnny continued to remain encouraged! She used to profess: "God got it!!!!" Johnny taught me; how to retain strength! She would say: "Belle, just believe God; you will be okay!" I will be forever grateful to Johnny! She spent countless hours; pouring her oil into this vessel. Thank you, Johnny Ruth.

 Another sister in Christ; Carolyn Rubin, had come to my ministry. We became friends; after, her initial visit to the church. She possessed endurance and faith. As a result, both my endurance, and faith have tremendously increased! As my sister in Christ battled with the illness; she never stopped professing Jesus. When everything around her looked dim; she knew how to light up the room. I literally watched my precious sister endure pain. Although, she never complained. Her bravery helped me to understand: it does not matter how deep you are in the valley. God's hand will never be too short.

In summation, Flora Griffin, Carolyn Rubin, and Johnny Ruth's faith caused me; to continue to go on, no matter what. I dedicate this book to the victors; who have gone on before me. They were survivors; because, they never lost hope! They never stopped believing in God! He can do it!

Made in the USA
Columbia, SC
19 March 2022